The Talk:

Vital Expressions

and

Conversations

by

Families of Color

The Talk

The Talk: Vital Expressions and Conversations

by Families of Color

© Garden of Neuro Publishing February 2023

Published in Poughkeepsie New York U.S.A.

ISBN 979-8-9851332-5-7 Paperback

Publishing Consultant: Lisa Tomey-Zonneveld, Manager Prolific Pulse Press LLC

The Talk

Epigraph v

Acknowledgements vii

These Words viii

Introduction xi

Juntu Ahjee 1

   The Emasculation of Black Fathers in America 1

Kimberly Bolden 9

   DON'T SLEEP 9

Yasmin S. Brown 14

   I Am My Community 14

   I Can't Breathe 17

Angelica Chapman 21

   My Beautiful Black Boy 21

Carla M. Cherry 26

   Shield 26

   Dear Kimani, ... 30

   A Different Beast 34

Chyrel J. Jackson 38

   Hands in Plain Sight 38

Zaneta Varnado Johns 42

   My Talk with Jerron-1997 42

Another Talk: Helping Others 45

Alshaad Kara 50

Racism 50

Marriage 51

Love problems 52

C. Miller 55

Texas weather is so unpredictable. 55

LaMia Michele Pierce 60

A Dinner Conversation For Black Families 60

LaVan Robinson 70

Why? 70

Fleecing Of The Innocents 72

Richa Dinesh Sharma 75

The first conversation till the last... 75

Darryl Varnado 81

The Talk, a Grandfather's Perspective 81

Lyris D. Wallace 90

Living While Black 90

What is your story? 96

Resources 112

Epigraph

Our watchword has been "the land of the free and the home of the brave." Brave men do not gather by thousands to torture and murder a single individual, so gagged and bound he cannot make even feeble resistance or defense. Neither do brave men and women stand by and see such things done without compunction of conscience, nor read of them without protest.

—**Ida B. Wells-Barnett**, political journalist, teacher, 1900

The fight is not just being able to keep breathing. The fight is actually to be able to walk down the street with your head held high — and feel like I belong here, or I deserve to be here, or I just have [a] right to have a level of dignity.

—**Alicia Garza**, civil rights activist, cofounder of Black Lives Matter movement, 2015

Sixty-five years have passed, and I still remember the face of young Emmett Till. ... Despite real progress, I can't help but think of young Emmett today as I watch video after video after video of unarmed Black Americans being killed, and falsely accused. My heart breaks for these men and women, their families and the country that let them down—again.

The Talk

My fellow Americans, this is a special moment in our history. Just as people of all faiths and no faiths, and all backgrounds, creeds and colors banded together decades ago to fight for equality and justice in a peaceful, orderly, nonviolent fashion, we must do so again.

—**John Lewis**, U.S. congressman, civil rights icon, 2020

Acknowledgements

Special Thank Yous for those who worked with us to make this the best possible book.

First of all to all the contributors for their strong, heart rich words.

Chyrel J. Jackson for her guidance with the cover design and over all support for this project.

Carla Cherry for selecting the epigraph, finding just the right words to start off this collection.

Zaneta Varnado Johns for providing resource information and for reviewing the poet laureate poem as well as assisting with the journal pages.

The Talk

These Words

As a loving parent
I read these words
opened my mind
expanded my soul
to take these words in
thankful that
in addition
to the words I still say
to my adult child
I do not have to say

These words
within *The Talk*

Every loving parent
knows to give safety advice
to their children
but these words
these words in *The Talk*
these are not the words
white people have to instill in our children

The Talk

Thank you to people of color
who paused to share
these words of wisdom
for survival
for enlightenment to the world at large
it is my hope
my deepest desire
that after reading these words
they will stick in the minds
of people who do not have to say them
since we are among the reasons
these words must be said

These words
are words
for life

Lisa Tomey-Zonneveld
Garden of Neuro Institute Poet Laureate 2022-23

The Talk

Introduction

He was born in Jamaica. With short locs. He admitted that he doesn't look like the typical Jamaican, and when I asked him why he said that, he told me that his skin is darker than most Jamaicans. *Ah—I see,* I told him, and that started us off on a conversation about Trevor Noah. He'd never heard of Trevor Noah. I guess following comedians is a luxury that many people don't have.

He had come to stay at my AirBnB, to do some work and save some money. The room he stayed in was inexpensive and affordable for him, and he had a goal— pay off some bills.

I later learned in a conversation with his father that he was doing so well—attending the local community college here, five minutes from my home, and working with people who were supporting him in creating a good life for himself. He got good grades. He was studying chemistry. The college community thought he had a promising future.

The week just prior, one of the other residents here—I have two housemates who also came here through AirBnB, and later requested to live here as tenants— texted me overnight and said, Susan, Maurice has been just sitting in a chair all night, staring off into space, and occasionally talking to himself.

The Talk

That didn't seem all that odd to me—apart from the sitting in a chair all night part— I often talk to myself for extended periods.

So because my housemates flagged his behavior, I took a seat on the couch next to where he sat in a chair, and I started a conversation.

"Hey Maurice, you okay? What's going on?"

Maurice looked off to the left, to the right, mumbled a few words, then looked at me. Almost as if the sound waves just took a little longer to reach his brain.

A coherent sentence came out, but honestly, I don't know what it was.

I listened as he drifted in and out of sense-making and non-sense making. A bit like what you or I might do after waking up suddenly after a very deep sleep.

I could see that he was sometimes with me, connected in conversation, and sometimes, not. I remembered conversations like this I'd had with my grandmother, who had dementia at the end of her life. Sometimes there. Sometimes not there. It was obvious that something was going on, not typical, not normal. It was something undeniably different, if you just engaged in a conversation for a few short minutes.

But Maurice was a young man. He wasn't at the end of his life. This was not dementia.

The Talk

I asked, "Maurice, do you take any medications?" He answered, "yes."

Now I had his full attention. "Did you take your medication today?"

"No."

"Why not Maurice?"

"I don't like the way they make me feel. They don't make a difference."

"When was the last time you took your meds, Maurice?"

He looked up at the ceiling, trying to remember. There was a long pause.

"Maurice, do you have your medications here in your room?"

He answered yes.

"Could you go get the bottle for me please?"

"Yes," he said, and he got up out of the chair, probably for the first time in many hours, and went off to retrieve the bottle. It's funny what any human will do when given a mission.

A few moments later, he returned with the bottle. I took a look at it. I noticed that he didn't get distracted. He went on his mission, retrieved the subject article, and came right back.

I thanked him, as he sat back down in the comfortable chair he'd spent the evening in. Everyone says it's the most comfortable chair in the house. Even if it does look a little frumpy and worn.

I went to the kitchen, noting the date the prescription was filled. Only just recently. I opened the bottle and counted the number of tablets inside. I calculated how many should be missing. Apparently, it had been just two days since he had not taken his meds.

I sat down again in front of him, and asked him again why he stopped taking them. Same answer. "They aren't working."

I replied, looking him in the eye, as his gaze was also fixed on my face, "That's not true Maurice. You've been here for two weeks now. I notice the difference since you stopped taking them. You are different now than you were last week or the week before."

He considered that for a long moment.

I went on. "Will you take your medicine for me, right now?"

"Yes," he calmly and softly replied.

The Talk

I stood up and went for a glass of water, coming back to hand him the glass and his pill.

He took it without a fuss. No objections.

We sat there for a bit, and I thought about what I should do next. I had no immediate idea. I'd never actually been confronted with a person having the beginnings of a schizophrenic break before.

A thought popped into my head. The weather was gorgeous. It was the end of May. The beginnings of summer, late spring. The sky was a beautiful blue and the clouds were big and puffy. "Let's go outside," I said.

We both got up and went out to visit my vegetable garden. Maurice readily followed me.

I started to pull some weeds. He started to help me. I went and got a wheelbarrow. We started to throw weeds into the barrow. While we worked side by side, he started to tell me stories of what it was like to grow up in Jamaica. What the elementary schools were like. How the children, and the people in the community, treated him. They were the stories that anyone would share about those incidents that still loom large in our lives, years and decades after we've experienced them.

So we weeded. We shared stories. We enjoyed the sun and the breezes. Maurice took his shoes and socks off and stood barefooted against the rich garden soil. I thought about how we are connected. To all of it, and everything. To each other. I prayed a little silent prayer, saying, okay, God, if you want me to host this young man who happens to be challenged in this way, for a little bit longer, I'm down. I can handle anything you throw at me, because I know you won't give me anything I'm not ready for.

We stayed that way, communing in story and with nature, for about an hour. Then we went inside.

I cooked a big breakfast for Maurice. Eggs and toast and OJ and fried potatoes. I served him a giant plate. He was happy and grateful and finished every last bite.

I thought all was right with the world again.

But I was mistaken.

Later that day, Maurice went to work. He was driving for Uber.

I never saw Maurice again. I wondered what happened and where he'd gone.

A few days later, news came on the air. George Floyd had been killed by police in a horrible display of violence.

Afterwards, I received a message from AirBnb. Would it be okay for Maurice's parents to contact me? I said yes, of course. They could share my information with them.

xvi | P a g e

The Talk

Two days later, Maurice Senior called me, old school, on the telephone. He was asking if they could pick up Maurice's things. I answered, of course, no problem, but there wasn't much here. Just the pair of socks that he'd taken off that day we gardened. And a prescription bottle with his medicine in it.

"What happened to Maurice? Is he okay?"

"He's dead," came the reply.

I felt my legs turn to rubber and I had to sit down. I couldn't believe what I was hearing.

We shared some moments of grief together. I shared with Maurice Senior the stories of Maurice's last days with me, and how sweet these memories were. He was grateful to hear the stories.

I offered my assistance, if there could be any. In the days that followed, all anyone could talk about was George Floyd. But Maurice had been shot 5 times by a New Jersey State Police officer just days before Floyd's murder, and his name was buried in the small town press. Friends of mine were able to track down small notices and press about the case. For many months after this happened, every place I saw a posting that said "Say Their Name," I requested they also write Maurice Gordon's name on their banners and posters. I was determined to not let his name disappear.

The Talk

But we know that there are thousands if not millions of names that have vanished into the sea of obscurity when it comes to the death of black lives in America. What could one person do to make a difference?

This was the question I asked myself. And that was the birth of the idea about this book called, "The Talk." I thought, if only white folk could know what it felt like to care for someone who you know in your heart is every day at risk for senseless murder, just by virtue of the color of their skin. What must that feel like? Can we open a window into this reality, for others to try to understand?

My friend Nanci Arvizu says, "it doesn't affect you until it affects you." Maurice Gordon's life affected me. I will never forget him or his story. My hope is that our anthology "The Talk" – both this volume and the ones that follow – will plant the seeds in peoples' hearts that grow to nourish the love and compassion we need to make a difference, so that we can prevent senseless murders like these in the future.

Heart to heart – let's share our stories.

Susan Brearley, Founder, Garden of Neuro Institute

Juntu Ahjee

The Emasculation of Black Fathers in America

There is a negative stereotype of African American males which falls into a disparaging narrative of social acceptance. Mainstream media is one of many evil entities who perpetuate influence on the public's perception regarding men of color. Those of many, who oppose the ratcheted system that tries to oppress the foundation of good, upstanding men, are usually put in a category of failure. People tend to judge or criticize the exterior of presence, instead of embellishing the character of a person's countenance. In the eyes of man, we are not created equal. In the eyes of God, there is only one man.

During the treachery of slavery, a vast majority of African American families were separated or divided at slave auctions, forced into incestuous assimilation, or just brutally tortured as a sport. At the core of it all, were black mothers making unimaginable sacrifices to keep their families together. What goes unnoticed or unmentioned, on many occasions, is the durability that black fathers embodied during a time when pride was an automatic death sentence. It's the duality of man. Sometimes pride can outweigh the will of those who try to oppress you. If you can destroy a man's pride, a part of his soul will deplete away. Unfortunately, many black fathers were broken spiritually and emotionally as a result of that loss of pride. Try to imagine being held captive against your will, outnumbered by sadistic parasites who hate you, engaging in the most vile, animalistic sexual acts with your wife and children (girls and boys), who could also be sold at any given time, and resistance on your behalf will result in public humiliation. Make no mistake; many male slaves were sodomy raped as well. Stripped naked, chained to trees and bull whipped in front of their families. Only the strong survive, but a man's pride never dies. Could the obsession of pride lead to the disparity of his own bondage? It is one of the seven deadly sins which victimize every man.

In the many decades, since the abolishment of slavery, African American fathers were the pillars in the black community. Every man is a father in some shape or form. Whether it's a schoolteacher, pastor, policeman, mailman or ice cream vendor, these figures represented guidance among many urban youths. We cannot, however, ignore or debunk the long-term toxic effects attributed from the atrocities of slavery. It transcends generationally from a diseased mindset. If you don't know where you come from, how can you know who you are?

A prophecy of the existence of man knows his purpose. His purpose in life, love, freedom, and destiny are connected to his well-being. A sense of direction without a map of guidance only leads to no destination. For many Black men and fathers in America, the road to sovereignty meets at the crossroads towards a dead end. There is no good in being misunderstood; those who praise understand none who gave. Black fathers (who care) are among the most disrespected.

It is foretold through history, from various anthropologists and scientists, that the first body of man was discovered in Africa. People of melanated skin texture originated from this region. God created man from the beginning of time. Thus, through controversial analysis, would it be fair to suggest that indigenous stages of sin started with men of color? Did we perpetuate our heathenness doom? In the context we currently know as 'power' was befallen upon the original man. A man accepts responsibility for his mistakes, a fool will continue to create mistakes, but a king will rectify those mistakes. As an original man in the eyes of God, we are held highly accountable for our transgressions. Black men, strong alpha males cannot continue to play the victim among the enemy who oppresses us. If you think of yourself as a king, you will rise up and stabilize circumstances which threaten to destroy your existence. Unfortunately, the abundance of beta males will become subservient and follow those who pacify their own weaknesses. A true original man will accept responsibility for his actions.

The Talk

As we currently face future adversity, Black families are divided at a massive level of proportions. A plethora of disagreements, jealousy, and anger have put lethal (if not sometimes) unforgiving boundaries against each other. In the center of this madness is the absence of Black fathers or strong Black males being prevalent in the family and the community. Many of our brothers are institutionalized, uneducated, uninformed, and unloved. This is just a small ingredient that is applied through white supremacy to keep hatred among our people seasonal. Hate is like fire; it must be fed for it to spread. Love is water; it must spread for it to grow. We cannot grow as a harvest if we (along with the enemy) plant thorns and weeds in the garden. It is applicable through progressions of humanity from then until now. Growth comes with time; time only ends when you decease to grow. God blesses those who create and condemns those who destroy. Black fathers were born to blossom.

The continuity of the path towards solidarity travels on the righteous soul who seeks it. Many crooked trails are followed and explored. The journey of a Black life is quite a distance from the birth of pain; we differ from culture, but the pursuit of happiness ends towards the same destination regardless of who you are. As a Black father, I have failed in more than many ways. If I live to see a million more sunrises and sunsets, I will give an eternity to spend one sunny day with my children.

The Talk

In a world as corrupt as if the devil were blessed with absolute authority, Black fathers, let's remember we are prophets of the alpha and omega. We continue to fight monumental battles at the forefront of nucleus prejudice. Even as the war continues, battles are determined on influence; endurance decides victory. Black fathers will be triumphant in the suicidal justice noose they try to hang us with. THEN, and only then, will we be able to find comradely amongst ourselves who are heavily indoctrinated to a covenant of righteousness. We may be broken, but never defeated.

In remembrance of my father SSGT G. Gutter Sr.

Juntu Ahjee, often imitated but never duplicated. Originally born in the Midwestern region, the youngest son of a decorated soldier, his father and his mother was a nurse. As a child, Juntu showed tremendous interest in writing stories. In the late 70s, he became a huge horror fan and began creating his own horror stories, which got him in trouble in school. As a teen, he developed an art of storytelling to keep himself out of the penal system. During the 80s, he was an honor student and received many accolades and scholar awards. In the 90s, he indulged in social mentorship for African American youths. He also became a father during this time. Juntu's writing endeavors would end at a standstill for several years due to life's unexpectancies. In 2000, he relocated to Seattle, WA. After connecting with family, he became a ghost writer in the Hip-Hop scene. He soon formed a group with some friends called, 'Society's Child'. They recorded songs reflecting racial injustice and political corruption. In 2010, Juntu took a strong interest in poetry. This led to him pursuing a career as an author and a screenwriter. In 2020, he published his first novel, the action crime drama, 'The Legend of Sister Hattie Harris'. Later the same year, he published the follow up 'The Return of Sister Hattie Harris'. He has two poetry books, 'Ebonology and Ebonology Book Two' published in 2021. And the family comedy-drama, 'Papa's Boys' published in 2021. As of 2022, Juntu has three completed screenplays in pre-production, a podcast, and an up-and-coming YouTube channel geared to help Black entrepreneurs, authors and finding missing children. As Juntu would say, "you are the author of your own story, embrace every chapter!"

Who am I?

Upon reflection what are my privileges?

_____

_____

_____

_____

_____

_____

_____

_____

_____

_____

_____

_____

_____

_____

_____

_____

_____

_____

_____

_____

_____

_____

_____

Kimberly Bolden

DON'T SLEEP

Seems they count dollars
like insomniacs count sheep
while we count bodies
Don't sleep
or run
or walk
For God's sake don't look up or down
or drive
Don't stumble
Walk slow
Hands up
Dignity down
Don't smile
Don't frown
Be apathetic and apologetic
No, keep your mouth shut
Don't flinch
Don't resist, confess or plead the fifth
Don't reach for a gun that doesn't exist
or your license
Make no sudden moves
If you do there will be checks processed
in the name of the law

The Talk

Vacations taken
Book deals made
and smoking guns auctioned off for millions
While your family seeks donations
to make funeral arrangements
and the community groans and moans
and morns your untimely demise
White supremacists will rally
to financially support the culprit,
murderer, domestic terrorist
Don't sleep
like an insomniac on speed
Proceed slowly but don't move
Whatever you do
Stay woke for hours on end
Days upon days
Because you might be mistaken for a thug
Determined to be disagreeable
before one syllable leaves your lips
No reconcile when being profiled
for driving while black
Don't sleep
because if you sleep
you might not make it back
Don't sleep
because you may be awakened by gunshots and cha-
chings

The Talk

Jackpots jumping in the form of pensions and early
retirement
Paid suspension
No arrest
No indictment
Don't sleep
Like an insomniac on crack
Don't fall back
Don't choke
Stay up
Stay woke

Kimberly "DuWaup" Bolden is an artist with a range of talents who has been bringing her brand of flavor to the art scene for twenty years. With five independent albums, an artist development company, and a highly sought-after poetry slam, DuWaup's Cincinnati Poetry Slam, DuWaup is also a published author. Her debut poetry book titled, "SINCERELY, DuWaup" (Shuga Shuga Publishing, LLC) is accompanied by her first digitally distributed audio recording project, titled "SINCERELY, DuWaup the Soundtrack" (Thunda Grownd Productions, LLC).

The story I would stand on a stage to tell ...

_____

_____

_____

_____

_____

_____

_____

_____

_____

_____

_____

_____

_____

_____

_____

_____

_____

_____

_____

_____

_____

_____

_____

The Talk

Yasmin S. Brown

I Am My Community

I am my community.... My community is me

My Black grandson

My Black brother and

My Black father

I am my community......My community is me

My Black granddaughter

My Black sister and

My Black mother

I am my community....... My community is me

We are not a threat to you

As you are to me

We want peace and justice

Is that too hard to see

The Talk

I am my community......My community is me

I stand and fight for humanity

To take flight

I am my community....... My community is me

We stand

Against racism

Economic injustice

Murder and chaos

I am the boss......The boss of accountability

I hold you accountable for what we see

Presidents

Mayors

Governors

Senate and congress

We are your community

I know you see us

The Talk

Open your eyes and look to the skies

God is telling you to see me

I know you do!

The black

The green

The red and yellow

I know you see me

I see you

The lying

The cheating

The invading my free will

I am my community......My community is me

I stand before you

As my community stands with me

As we yell, I am my community.... My community is me!

The Talk

I Can't Breathe

The noose is getting tighter.... Gasp! Gasp!

Cut the rope, cut the rope.... Release

A community's peace

When we stop protesting in these streets

The streets where needs of all ethnicities are complete

Complete with equality

Yes, we are still fighting for equality to be given

We are driven to declare and share

This world with the same rights

we no longer must fight

Fight to drive

Fight to walk

Fight to run

In all neighborhoods

Neighborhoods that do not look like me

The Talk

Neighborhoods where I should not fear

Swinging from a tree.... A tree of strange fruit

The fruit from the dreadful forbidden tree

Steadfast we are still on our knees

Praying every day for the right to safely live in peace

and not just say goodbye in these streets

Yasmin S Brown is a healthcare professional with a gift of compassion and empathy. She focuses on women being the pillars of their communities as well as their mental health. Through her literacy, leadership, and life coaching her creative expression inspires entrepreneurs/authorpreneurs looking to make an impact on the world.

How would I define peace and justice?

Angelica Chapman

My Beautiful Black Boy

My Beautiful Black Boy
I love when they count you out
My Boy
Discover yourself without doubt
Learn and grow, find what brings you joy
Some people may pout
My Boy, you can't please everybody for clout
I believe in you golden boy.
Don't let no one tell you,
"Timeout, you can't be this because of that, boy."
Believe in your belief and love what you're about.
You are the chief of overjoy.
Achieve without doubt.
You can be a schoolboy, ball boy, bat boy, tomboy,
carboy, cowboy, office boy, drummer boy,
mother's boy, and boy scout.
You don't have to be one dimension, My Boy.
You are joy.
I am happy for you throughout.
So repeat after me, "This is me and I'm blessed."
You are not a decoy.
It is okay to cry out.
Be brave using your mind.

The Talk

Be strong using your heart.
Use the energy of fear as fuel
My Boy, Breakout
You can get it while eating ramen noodles, golden boy.
Money trees are the perfect tree for shade, so lookout.
My Boy, breathe 1, 2, 3, 4
You're going to be alright
Keep your head up high and your dreams far-out.
This is what I call love, My Boy.
I'm happy for you throughout.
My Beautiful Black Boy.

The Talk

Angelica Chapman is a health and wellness advocate committed to helping others improve their lives and develop healthy living habits. She first developed an interest in health and wellness as a young girl, and during high school, she studied to become a certified nursing assistant before attending North Carolina State University.

Like many of the individuals she works with, Angelica has struggled with her health and wellbeing. She's a busy professional, entrepreneur, wife, and mom and understands first-hand how difficult it can be to find a balance between a career, family, and healthy lifestyle. After years of neglecting her health, Angelica discovered the tools, strategies, and support she needed to make long-lasting and meaningful changes in her life. Now she's dedicated to using her platform to share health and fitness related tips, tricks, and tools and help individuals combat everything from unhealthy eating habits to health conditions like hypertension, which can lead to serious and fatal heart problems if left untreated. Many of the techniques Angelica shares focus on making small changes like taking the time to breathe or reducing sodium intake to help individuals see that their journey to health and wellbeing doesn't need to feel overwhelming or impossible. In addition to helping hundreds of people create healthy habits, Angelica has also had her journey and successes featured in multiple publications throughout her career, including the Greensboro News and Record and, most recently, Voyage Raleigh.

In her spare time, Angelica enjoys spending time with her family, volunteering in her community, hiking, traveling, photography, doing yoga and being a compassionate awareness advocate.

What words come to mind to describe your child?

_____

_____

_____

_____

_____

_____

_____

_____

_____

_____

_____

_____

_____

_____

_____

_____

_____

_____

_____

_____

Carla M. Cherry

Shield

I.

I am shaking, wiping my eyes
during the viewing of the
The Central Park Five at Abyssinian.
I think of my son. My students.
The year before, in 2012,
after Trayvon was murdered,
we had an assembly about racial injustice
at my school.
It is on the same campus
Kevin Richardson attended briefly before
his conviction.
When asked
if they had been stopped and frisked,
most of our students,
Black and Brown,
raised their hands.

Korey Wise, Kevin Richardson,
and Yusef Salaam are on the panel.
I stand,
say how happy I am to see them free

The Talk

and I always believed in their innocence.
We line up to greet them.
I ask Yusef Salaam if it is OK to hug him.
He consents.
I ask if he can come speak to my students.
He gives me the number to The Innocence Project.

II.
I was a senior in high school when Ms. Meili was raped.
I prayed as cameras flashed in the faces of
Raymond
Kevin
Anton
Kharey
Yusef
wolf pack
wildin'
GUILTY
before the trial began.

In my Human Condition class, my teacher Dr. M.
listed pejoratives

savages
animals

across the blackboard.

The Talk

Which one of those words best described the Central Park Five?

One of two Black students in that class,
I was the only one to object.

III.
I called The Innocence Project.
Kevin Richardson and Raymond Santana came to our assembly.
They answered every question about the documentary,
from students and staff.
Ate lunch with us,
students spellbound as Raymond described
the violence he witnessed in prison
how he protected himself,
how the system is set up to devour.

Students went home and told their parents about the forum.
One of my students bought the book *The Central Park Five* and read it.

IV.
I called colleagues
the day I saw Eric Garner murdered online.

The Talk

Why should our students believe
in the transformative power of education?

We formed a committee,
planned a school-wide forum, "Know Your Rights".

A panel discussion with attorneys one week.
A Town Hall, the second.

Fruitvale Station,
and open discussion.

There was half a row of students who were sulking
or crying.

They said were friends or classmates
of Kimani Gray.

The Talk

Dear Kimani,

When I saw our students crying over you,
I wished I could have met you. Seen you smile.

I know you traveled an hour every day to get to
Urban Assembly School for Design and Construction in
Manhattan,

that you attended every day, but sometimes your mother
had to throw cold water on you to get you out of bed.

If you had been in my school, in my class,
I would have called you by your nickname, Kiki.

I would have bought you a cupcake
when you turned sixteen.

"Oh, you're from Brooklyn? East New York? Cool,"
I would have said, and crossed my arms to represent for
the BX.

I hope you would have told me about yourself
in one of the personal essays I assign,

that you would have told me you were the sixth child in
your family.
That your mother came here from Jamaica.

The Talk

On Open School Night, your mother might have told me that
though you smiled a lot, you had a broken heart.

Your oldest brother Jahma, who checked your homework,
bought you clothes, kept you out of the streets,

was killed in a car accident
two years before.

I am sorry your family had to live in a shelter for a while.
I know you were missing Jahma when you started hanging
out in the streets,

were arrested a few times–
joyriding, a ruckus at McDonalds, truancy.

But I would have loved for you to write about the day
your mother was smiling, shaking keys to your family's
new four-bedroom duplex,

and how you jumped at the ceiling.
Your very own bedroom.

The Talk

How excited you must have been on March 9,
a few days after you all moved in.

A Sweet Sixteen.
You probably took a little extra time in the mirror. For
the Ladies.

The last thing on your mind would have been
plain-clothes officers jumping out of a car

ordering you, other teens on the way to that party
to stop for questioning.

The Kiki my students cried over could not have
pointed a .38 at the officers.

I am so sorry they shot at you eleven times.
I cannot imagine how it felt to be hit by seven bullets.

The front and back of your body.
Witnesses say you were not armed.

You were trying to fix your baggy pants,
maybe flee when you were shot.

The Talk

It was kind of your principal to write a letter to your
family,
and say that for the year and a half that you were at that
school,
they got to see your best self.
But that was yet to come, had you been allowed to grow
up.

A Different Beast

Ramarley Graham lived
twenty minutes to the west of us.

Because I cannot wish away a world where
most white mothers never worry
if their sons will be chased home by cops,
shot in front of their little brothers or grandmothers,
who are threatened to be shot too,
as the system fails to prosecute,

because abiding laws,
a loving family
and manners
will not suffice if you have Black skin,

I bring Khari to a forum facilitated
by Black law enforcement officers,
"What do you do if you are stopped by the police?"

You have the right to remain silent.
You do not have to consent to a search but if they suspect a
weapon they can search you anyway.
Stay calm.
Keep your hands where the police can see them.
Do not run, resist, or obstruct the officers in their duties.
Do not lie or give false documents.

The Talk

should not be litany
for Black boys and men

I pray Khari has it memorized
every time he leaves the house.

Carla M. Cherry's poetry has appeared in *Random Sample Review*, *Anti-Heroin Chic*, *433*, *Raising Mothers*. A Best of the Net and Pushcart Prize nominee, her five books of poetry are available via iiPublishing. She holds an M.F.A. in Creative Writing from the City College of New York.

When strangers look at you, what do you hope they see? When I look at strangers am I judgmental?

_____

_____

_____

_____

_____

_____

_____

_____

_____

_____

_____

_____

_____

_____

_____

_____

_____

_____

_____

The Talk

Chyrel J. Jackson

Hands in Plain Sight

We won't speak today of birds and bees.

I won't tell you to beware of fast girls hiding behind trees
speaking softly to
you of nature beckoning sweet honeybees.

Today my little boy's innocence will be lost
in a different way.

Lord, give me wisdom tell me what to say.

How do I tell him White Police officer's
won't protect him.

No at eight years old Peace officers are not
a Black boy or Black man's friend.

I have to tell him always keep your hands in plain sight.

Son, Black skin is used for target practice for the men
that wear blue any day and all through the night.

The Talk

Avert direct eye contact be mindful of your tone.

Don't ever raise your voice, you may not return home.

Yes sir, no sir, do I have permission
to retrieve my ID sir?

Son, do you understand?

No sudden movements keep your hands in plain view.
Left hand at 10, right hand at 2.

Maybe with a lot of faith and prayer when
you're stopped by police perhaps they'll
reconsider killing you.

The Talk when you are Black never comes with ease.

In 2022 It means stay away from cops so you're not shot
by profiling, racist, White, police.

Black parenting is hard a hurt of a different sort
our kids skin color won't protect them,
for some it's an unnecessary curse.

Always keep your hands in plain sight.
Maybe if you're lucky son, they'll return you home safely
to your family tonight.

Chyrel J. Jackson is a Literary visionary. Reared in the South Suburbs outside Chicago. African American Literature influenced her writing and is one of her favorite genres. Jackson writes in the spirit of her past great Literary ancestors. 2021 garnered Chyrel her very first literary nomination, Pushcart Nominee-Poem Love Unspoken, Published in Heart Beats Anthology.

Along with her sister, Lyris D. Wallace, they published Mirrored Images and Different Sides of the Same Coin. This edgy writing duo appears in over 8 published poetry Anthologies. You will find them always writing. Creating written legacies one book at a time. Jackson is one writer that has found her poetic voice. You can find her on Sistersrocnrhyme.com

The first time I realized that safety is not a privilege that everyone enjoys...

_____

_____

_____

_____

_____

_____

_____

_____

_____

_____

_____

_____

_____

_____

_____

_____

_____

_____

_____

_____

The Talk

Zaneta Varnado Johns

My Talk with Jerron-1997

New house, new town, new hopes
Old stigma, old pains, old fears!

"Hey Ma, I'm going for a run," said Jerron
"No, not yet, let's talk," I cautioned
I thought of others who were taunted—
some even killed while going for a run...
"We just moved here. No one knows us.
The sun will soon set...
Not yet Son, not just yet!"

It was 1997—no cell phones—no protests—
Just a mother's knowing
"You are seventeen, a promising young man to me
To them, you are an imposing black figure—
a threat—someone to fear
They don't want you here!
To them, your life has little value
To me, prejudice is a serious matter!"

"Son, I see you, an honor student
A star athlete with a heart of gold

The Talk

They see breaking news—headlines
with threatening black images in the stories told
I see my only son, my pride and my joy
They see someone unequal—insist on calling you, "Boy."
I see my college bound student who excels in science
and math
They see a scary dark figure approaching them
on the path
I see a fine young man whose body is his temple
They see someone to harm and call it accidental
I see a bright future, a future attorney in fact
They see nearly two-hundred pounds—
strong, dangerous, and Black."

"So, I can't say *yes* to your run just yet
I love our new home and life
but our new city– we have to vet.
You see, our dilemma is wrong and so unfair
You have only one life, no extra to spare

For you, society offers no benefit of the doubt—just
doubt

For others, the privilege is two-fold, at least
For you, work twice as hard—like a beast

The Talk

For others, 'Get out of the car' means *Let me help you*
For you, the approaching siren signals a risky pursuit."

"Remember a full tank, working lights,
and active signals are must
Don't speed, don't swerve, above all, don't trust!
Draw no attention to your car
A traffic stop might go too far
Should you ever be pulled over,
make no sudden moves
Hands up, follow orders, respond as the officer rules."

"I'm sorry I can't guarantee
that my advice will always work
Each time I think of it, my heart breaks and hurts
No mother should have to worry
about her child with the police
After all, don't we pay them
to be officers of the peace!"

Another Talk: Helping Others

My son and I had many talks, especially about the way in which society views him. As a young Black man, it was important to discuss America's sometimes-not-so-protective order of police. He was conditioned to realize this unfortunate construct, knowing that he should never—intentionally or carelessly—draw negative attention to himself.

On one particular night, my son remembered another talk—the talk about protecting women and treating them with the utmost respect. When a naked young white lady frantically approached his vehicle at 1:30 AM, without hesitation, he rescued her. She was running and yelling that her abusive boyfriend was chasing her. As she jumped into his vehicle, he covered her with his jacket. He never considered that driving with a strange naked white woman at that time of night could potentially place him in danger. For him, protecting the woman in distress was paramount. To him, her color was not a concern. Thankfully, he drove her to safety and successfully placed her in police custody without incident.

The Talk

Easily, this story could have ended quite differently.
I shudder to imagine the white lady in distress bearing the
name of *Carolyn Bryant Donham*.
I shudder to imagine her presenting a different account
after enjoying the warmth of my son's fine sport coat,
lined with his DNA, on her naked privileged white body.
I shudder to imagine the violent angry white suitor
bearing the name of *Travis McMichael*.
I shudder to imagine the victim—or her angry white
suitor—sharing a different account with a white
policeman bearing the name of *Derek Chauvin*!
God have mercy!

I shudder to imagine all the mothers whose sons suffered a
different outcome!
Goodwill gone bad... horrid images—a mother's
nightmare.
I shudder to imagine the countless mothers
bearing the name of *Mamie Elizabeth Till-Mobley*.
Those grieving mothers whose promising black or brown
sons encountered the determined and hateful
Donhams, McMichaels, and *Chauvins*
on their kind-hearted journeys.
I shudder at the atrocities occurring still
in our beautiful yet flawed country—the country
bearing the name of the *United States of America*!

The Talk

I am proud that my son remembered our *other* talk
     the one about compassion and love
     the one about protecting others
     the one about doing what is right.
As a knowing mother, on that particular night,
I am grateful that God remembered my Black son and sent
him home safely!

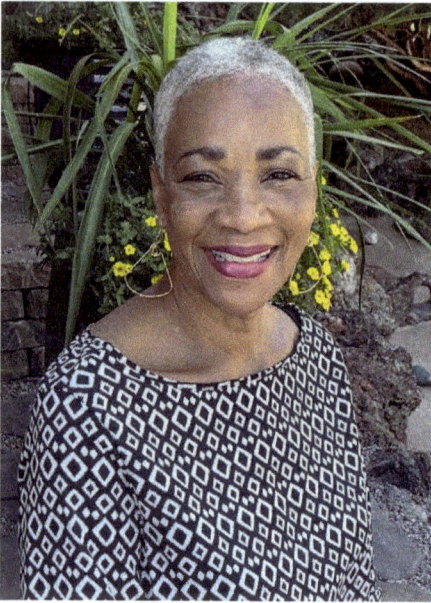

Zaneta Varnado Johns is a Pushcart Prize Nominee and 3-time bestselling author of *Poetic Forecast* and *After the Rainbow*. Johns is a contributing author in the Women Speakers Association's #1 international bestsellers *Voices of the 21st Century (2021 & 2022)*. Johns co-edited *Social Justice Inks* anthology with publisher Lisa Tomey-Zonneveld. She serves as an editor with the *Fine Lines Literary Journal* and administrator for the Passion of Poetry, an online platform for emerging and esteemed poets. Johns contributes to numerous anthologies and international literary publications. She is a retired human resources leader who resides in Westminster, Colorado, USA.

Website: zanexpressions.com

Times when it has been hard to let go...

_____
_____
_____
_____
_____
_____
_____
_____
_____
_____
_____
_____
_____
_____
_____
_____
_____
_____
_____
_____
_____
_____
_____
_____

The Talk

Alshaad Kara

Racism

I felt this stabbing ache,
In achieving this mortal heartache.

Up in the forbidden abode,
Unbeholden seas of tears appeared in every eye.

You are more prone to be caught, arrested, or beaten
around.

Tears of innocence did not suffice this deprivation,
As the societal conformity blew the wings of
righteousness away.

Human rights issues are always issued,
Because people of colour like me are deprived.

Up in the forbidden abode,
Unbeholden seas of tears appeared in every eye due to this
constant injustice.

The Talk

Marriage

Entice the heaven for a last haven,
Since the heart fell into an obligation of duty.

Arranging arranged marriages for everyone,
Love is ousted and likely to be forbidden.

This is the valediction of love,
Since my heart was inundated in the ravine of obligation.

Families keep talking about who is a more suitable match,
But no one listens to that brown heart of mine.

The Talk

Love problems

Dirty talks are forbidden.
The ironed heart is sponged in irony,
Since my confessions led to nightless conversations.

Letting the light burn the ties of attachment.
That leaves the compromises to colour it,
Internally the heart thought otherwise,
For a win of love.

But on the riskier side,
Destiny's circle led to another cycle of nightless sleep.

My heart had watered itself with cracks in its shadows,
Sadness in interest,
It had revived the vile past of its own heartbreak,
Of breaking ties with my family,
In my quest of love.

The Talk

Alshaad Kara is a Mauritian poet who writes from his heart. His latest poems were published in two anthologies, "Mille et une plumes" and "All Voices Heard Volume 1," in a collection of poems, "Italian Poems" and one journal, "Inlandia: A Literary Journey Fall 2022, Volume 13."

What conflicts did you notice in these poems that you can relate to?

_____
_____
_____
_____
_____
_____
_____
_____
_____
_____
_____
_____
_____
_____
_____
_____
_____
_____
_____
_____
_____
_____
_____

C. Miller

Texas weather is so unpredictable.

We roller-coaster. Climatic drops from 110° to freeze without time to prepare. Instructions go from, "make sure you're drinking plenty water" to "wear your hat and cover your ears" within days. When preparing my kids to go out in this weather these are the things I have to say.

But some climates never change.
Some temperatures can't be controlled.

Meteorologists have accepted the fact that there's a demographic set apart and there's no fair weather on their radar. Traumatizing tropical storms do irreparable harm and for this neck of the woods, that's the norm.

"What's the weather going to be like dad?" the question my youngest son asks.

Partly cloudy with a chance of pain is the prediction I always say. For black folks pain is inevitable, a part of our everyday.

When I tell him to cover his ears, it's said with fear and reservations knowing having a hoodie on for him, could

get him handcuffed. Locked up. Profiled and my child?
My child could be the next gloomy weather report on the
6 o'clock news. Told him to cover his ears, now I'm here
in tears singing the blues.

What if he panics and moves in haste when red and
blue lights flash in his face? It's cold outside son - and the
weather ain't changing no time soon. Dad can tell you to
prepare for hot or cold temperatures, but for us, when it
rains - it pours.

Politicians, preachers, pimps, and leeches - all 'hope' died
with CHRIST. Then they gave us pictures painting HIM
white, ain't no hope for this hopeless life. Hope hope hold
me while holding this mic, storm's brewing off the coast.

He brewing.

He ain't mad, sad, or speaking pridefully; he just doing
what a Hebrew do. He brewing. Gun fights and
stereotypes are what's in store for my child's black life.
Being misunderstood and profiled son is your lifelong
weather forecast, and as your dad I can honestly say,
"that's all that's in store for your black ass."

Why?

The Talk

Cause that's a fact. There are no sunny days, no fair weather on the doppler radar when you're black. Hurricanes of pain. Strong winds from the south that make us doubt whether black lives even matter at all. If black lives matter as much as yalls? The constitution prohibits the banning of slavery. There are still slaves today and America will still beat em. Treat em like they don't need em. Fool them into believing that they can march their way to freedom. Leave us writing painful poems knowing no one will ever read em.

It's cold outside son.

All we can do is cover up good, dress ourselves in mercy and prayer. From the time you wake til you fall back asleep, there's death and suffering everywhere. The toughest part of my everyday is when my children are away from home. Time after time, I stare at my phone screen wondering if I'll get a call saying they're gone.

Texas weather is so unpredictable
It changes from day to day
Partly cloudy with a chance of pain
Black folks weather don't neva change

Carlos Terrell Miller is a Hebrew humbled by life's experiences and personal choices. Serving as a speaker, author, dad, husband, publisher, and spoken-word artist, his moving messages continue to emphasize a rededication and recommitment to healing as men. The healing will enable us to further develop as positive, emotionally present husbands and fathers in homes all over the country.

A native of Jackson Mississippi, his career choices, including his 4 year military service, led him to his wife of 25 years and landed them both in Texas after completing their service.

"A community will never feel real men if the community does not help heal real men within", is one of his more noted slogans. His voice is one that communicates the necessity of male vulnerability, as well as brotherly understanding and supportive availability in the healing process, which is exemplified and encouraged in his writing.

What would I love to not have to say to you?

_____

_____

_____

_____

_____

_____

_____

_____

_____

_____

_____

_____

_____

_____

_____

_____

_____

_____

_____

_____

The Talk

LaMia Michele Pierce

A Dinner Conversation For Black Families

The opinions and views expressed within this essay are solely based on my personal viewpoints as a Black woman living in today's society. While they may be a little triggering, that is not my intent. I do believe the historians have gotten wrong and that there is room for BIPOC peoples to write a new story. While you may disagree, just entertain the thought that the words you are about to read could possibly change the narrative and rewrite a new story of being Black in America.

"There is nothing new under the Sun," Ecclesiastes 1:9

I am a daughter of a Black man
I am a sister of a Black man
I am an aunt to young Black men
I am the niece of a Black man
I have been a lover, nurturer to a Black man
I am the grandmother to a little Black boy
I am the granddaughter of a Black man
As a Black woman I am the portal to which all life exists.

As I continue to hear the stories of murder of black boys and girls, men and women around the world, I have an ache within my heart that feels like electrical shocks throughout the entirety of my body. While the evening news continues to play the atrocities, the genocide, the modern day lynching of black men, women, boys and girls, I can't help but to think why is this the same story of old continuously being told. As the world continues to evolve, why is it that the story of being Black in this world seems to never change?

Again there is nothing new under the Sun. African American, Black History has taught us this fact.

What is the agenda? What is the intent of these social constructs, even the construct of a superior and an inferior race that continues to push the agenda that Black Lives just don't matter?

As I began to write this excerpt, it took me down memory lane to when I was a little girl and the conversations of race that were held around the dinner table. Growing up in the inner city in a predominantly black neighborhood my first memory of encountering race superiority was when the Klu Klux Klan would march through our small city and I would watch in amusement from the front porch. I didn't ask questions, however conversations would take place at the dinner table of that day's events. While my grandmother never spoke a negative word that made me fear others that differed in skin color from my

The Talk

own, she did make it plain that they had a right to express their beliefs as did I. Other conversations were of how she and her mother worked tirelessly cooking, cleaning and washing clothes for white folks to make a living back in her day.

The main conversations at our dinner table were about religion, being a good person to everyone, showing love to those who possibly wouldn't love me back and to strive for greatness in everything that I do in life. That I was just as good as anyone else regardless of the color of my skin. The stories of racism and a superior race I learned from books and public school education. As I continue to hear and watch current day news stories, it reminds me of an earlier period of time that I only read about in books.. Why do these same narratives continue to replay today as if history has not changed? Like a broken record playing constantly on repeat.

Why do black mothers and fathers have to give instruction to their sons and daughters on how to behave if and when they are confronted by those whose duties are to serve and protect them? Or anyone whose skin color supposedly makes them superior to their own?
As I have vowed to change the narrative within my own family, the conversation that I feel needs to be had at my dinner table and others, veers from the script that society

has embedded within the impressionable minds of young
black children through public school education.
I believe that all black families, whether a single parent
household or not, need to begin with the true origins of
Black history, who they are and that their history does not
begin with slavery. That the melanin of their skin makes
them royalty by default. Although the world's account of
history will attempt to convince them that they are cursed
by God, that is far from the truth. I believe it should be a
priority to teach that greatness is embedded within their
blood from ancestors that built this America as well as
other mighty nations around the world. Black inventors
and financial literacy should be the topic of discussion, in
my opinion and not fear.

While my opinion and viewpoints will not change the way
that others perform or view the lives of Black people in
society, I would like to think it would change the way that
Black and brown people view themselves.

This year as my family and I gathered for Thanksgiving
dinner I made it a priority to not forget the indigenous
families that are not thankful for this day. I made it a
priority to say a prayer for those families and dispel the
true meaning of Thanksgiving day.

Proper education begins with allowing the truth to expose
the powerful lies that have been told and held as truths for

too long. For far too long those considered the minority have bought into a narrative that was not created for them to rise only to keep them in bondage and in a constant state of fear of an enemy that cannot win unless you give power to that enemy.

As I am writing these words the song by Yassin Bey, "I want black people to be free", continues to drop into my Spirit along with a pain in my heart. True freedom can only be obtained through the eyes of truth and not fear. History will always be an account of his story, but does that have to make it my story? Or the story that I have to continue to tell?

While these words do not erase what is occurring around us as far as black on black crime or lives lost at the hands of police and others of different racial ethnicities, is it a possibility that these words offer an opportunity for a new story to be told? A true story which can shift the mindset of a race of people who do not know who they are outside of what and who others have decided they should be.

Every black and brown child should know that the color of their skin is something they wear proudly, it is not a threat to those who fear them recognizing their true identity and true power.

The Talk

As I close, I want to end with these words that I have found to be true.
Fear is a powerful drug and when we teach our children to fear, we disempower them.

I believe that as a Black mother, aunt, sister, daughter, cousin, and friend we have to disassociate from the fear, inferiority complex, and ideology that has been imposed upon us for far too long. Most if not all the laws that are in place today came into fruition to keep those of "lower minority" groups enslaved. While Black lives matter has become a popular chant, black lives will only matter when Black lives matter to the entire race of black people.
It is time to dispel the lies with truth. Fear is a death warrant, an energy that continues to seep through the bloodline of BIPOC families that we keep passing down and giving it power to breathe. We have the power to change the narrative, once the conversations around the dinner table change to solution mode we will no longer be victims to a system that is designed to tell a fictionalized story. The color of Black skin is not a crime or a societal threat. Black skin is not a weapon. They only fear you when you know not who you are. And they fear the day you discover your truth and the truth shall set you free.

Unfortunately, the inhuman treatment and the consistent discrimination of BIPOC people isn't a new phenomena. Statistics and media continue to show the injustices and discriminatory policies that have been in place for minority races since the beginning of time. The constitution of America wasn't written with me as a Black woman, my ancestors, my children or my children's children in mind. I'm not sure if in my lifetime I will ever see a world that shows dignity, justice or compassion for those who resemble me. I was told as a child that it only takes one person to stand against injustice to change the world, to stand for what is right even if I have to stand alone. Maybe, one day I pray and if not, at least I did my part by instilling the truth within my bloodline and my stories will forever be told from generation to generation, leaving a strong legacy just from my expression of telling the story of why melanated skin is perceived as a threat. I just want all black people to be Free and freedom can only come from truth, not the false illusion of fear.

LaMia Michele Pierce is a native of the small city Chester, Pennsylvania located on the outskirts of Philadelphia, Pennsylvania. She is also a survivor of life that many fight to escape from the grips of impoverishment. As a young child her favorite hobby was reading and writing. These two hobbies allowed her the ability to escape from her childhood traumas, crime and drugs surrounding her. LaMia was always quiet, yet her mind and imagination were always at work dreaming of a life that she would one day live. One of her accomplishments was becoming a self-published author. Her first book of many to come is titled, "She Writes from the Heart." With a world of chaos and dysfunction surrounding her, she maintained a heart that loved the unlovable and allowed her to find beauty in the world. LaMia is still writing and publishing, her love of writing led her down a path of creating healing journals, affirmation cards and other tools to assist others to overcome the barriers of life. She resides in Atlanta, Ga with her daughter and two grandchildren. Besides making a name for herself as an

The Talk

Author, and the CEO of One Planted Seed Stationary, she is also a motivational speaker and a world changer.
Be sure to remember her name as she is making a way to change the narrative for young women, teen mothers, victims of domestic abuse, her culture and the world in general.

LaMia can be reached for speaking engagements and events by email at:
miamichele42@gmail.com
Social Media Handles:
Facebook: Author LaMia Michele
Instagram: _planted_seeds

Stories told around my dinner table...

_____

_____

_____

_____

_____

_____

_____

_____

_____

_____

_____

_____

_____

_____

_____

_____

_____

_____

_____

_____

_____

_____

_____

The Talk

LaVan Robinson

Why?

As the dark shroud of spilled blood and death fills and taints the sweetness of the living air. The inhabitants of this twilight zone nightmare go about their daily business dealing with the residual effects much to bear. Nothing that happens while residing hostage to the gun isn't by coincidence but done with subliminal intention and design even to methodically and systematically block the rays of the sun. Individuals are on edge and all it takes nowadays is something not beneficial to their living arrangements to set off the chaos of assumption. We're in an uncertain process and times of deadly consumption. Nothing from nothing surely is a terrible sign and leaves us all with the dust and lint of zero gain. Watch out everyone because on any given day it could be who you would least expect to bring the horrific destruction and unprecedented pain. Is this how in the history books and the great journals and annals of our existence we want to be truly remembered? Hold up, bang, bang, bang, there goes another one dead as loved ones for the fallen to frantically suffer and cry. Why is this happening? Why don't we as one humanity, overall stop this madness when it takes away joy, happiness and blessings and is so saddening? Why do we continue to feed into the ideology of lies which is fabricated and manifested to destroy souls and lives? These questions I often think about and I still can't figure why. Why is it more likely that by the hands of those who look very much like me I'm destined to die? I ask too, why can't we give love a try? Why why why?

Fleecing Of The Innocents

The hidden messages of hate are subliminally interwoven in plain sight through encryption within and all around in the fine details and fundamental principles of society. The pushing of the agenda of racism, discrimination, prejudice, separation, and injustice is high on the bucket list of priorities. Those that have eyes, let them see the turmoil, pain and grief behind the method and madness of the creation of the haves and have nots. The system is predicated on the capitalization of a nonexistent humanity and its part of growth within this very nation. I don't understand fully the rift between blacks and white literally. On paper the powerful collaboration is a work of pure artistic creativity figuratively. Why is it that on this great big planet called our home and Mother Earth we cannot coexist and live together peacefully? All you see around you while living, struggling, and barely surviving in their America is based on falsification of the facts of naturalization . This I want you all to know; That to accept their ways of evilness as those who paved the road with good intentions is one that's hell bound and bent. Those that have eyes please see this like it always has been - the continuation of the fleecing of the innocents.

The Talk

LaVan Robinson is a 13-year veteran, he has written poetry since high school. "LaLa" is Robinson's poet name. He states that he loves poetry and will use it to inspire people and bring them closer to God. LaVan has several poetry collections available on Amazon as well as contributions to anthologies and literary journals. You can find LaLa performing at open mics and on podcasts. He can be found on Facebook, Instagram, and Twitter.

How can we safely co-exist?

_____
_____
_____
_____
_____
_____
_____
_____
_____
_____
_____
_____
_____
_____
_____
_____
_____
_____
_____

The Talk

Richa Dinesh Sharma

The first conversation till the last...

...cannot be summed up in an essay or a poem. Such are the conversations between mother and child, between sisters, between friends and kindred spirits. They go on and on. It was so long ago that I am sure I carry more memories of it than my son. It was his beginning in a multi-racial school here in Singapore. Although we've been in a place where people of multiple ethnicities exist in a charming harmony, there's always that unconscious effort to connect with more of one's own ethnicity.

My son (let's call him R) moved from a predominantly Asian kindergarten to a school where a huge majority of children were expats of Caucasian origin. We never spoke much about it and with R being a shy child, we didn't prod him much and goad him to make new friends. In a matter of a few weeks, homemade his first friends. All three of them were the front runners of the class and shared similar hobbies of reading and going treasure hunting in the school grounds. It was all fun and games till one fine day he got home and asked me the most weird question, "How come, mumma, I am not as fair as you?". I was flummoxed and decided to think the answer through. I wanted to know where the idea of the color of the skin came from. "Are brown people...dirty?", he persisted as I fed him an after-school snack.

"Hmmmmphh!"I sat down with a long sigh.

"No, they are not dirty, as in we are not dirty. We're just different shades of wheat because we eat a lot of wheat in India...", I supplied a rather lame reasoning.

"They do too...", he informed me.

"We live in the tropics and thus our skin gets browned more by the sun and then it becomes an inherited trait over generations. The lighter skinned people generally live in the colder parts of the world where the sun is not too harsh and thus...they're lightly baked.", I said, "but why does it bother you so much? Did anyone say anything to you at the school?"

"No one said anything but why can't I have golden hair and white skin like my friends?"

"It's not like you can't have it...it's just how you are. And, honestly, very cute."

"I could be cute if I was fairer...", he added as an afterthought.

"Do your friends (Let's call them A and F) not love you as you are?"

The Talk

"A asked me why I was brown and my hair so black and then F told us that all Indians are like that."

"Did you feel bad about this discussion?"

"No, but F said I was a brunette like his elder sister...and I didn't like it because I felt like a girl. But, why don't I have a similar color to yours even?"

I realized that these children were forging some early bonds in their life and there's a lot of curious discussion about each other that may enable a degree of greater understanding and closeness towards each other.

I couldn't taint it with a label of racism, of color-based discrimination, of a bias that is not yet a part of their understanding of the world.

"I think you want to be lighter in skin because you want to feel closer to them, is that it?"

"I just...mumma...we are like brothers. They both look similar and I look different."

"It's alright to be different. Imagine if y'all grew up and you took them for a backpacking trip across India, how weird they'll feel and all of us feel weird and out of place at times and that's ok. Am I making sense to you?"

The Talk

Over the next few days, I told him all sorts of things about birds wielding different colors of feathers and still sharing the same skies, chocolate cupcakes being as delicious as vanilla ones, a zebra and a hippo being friends in his favorite movie.

Our conversation went on for days till one day he got home and showed me a christmas card that A had made for him. It showed a red-roofed house on which was parked Santa's sleigh and right in front of the house were three boys, gifts in a pile next to them, posing for a picture with Santa (the picture that A drew). All three boys were differently colored- yellow, pink and blue with lovely red mops of hair. It made me laugh because their T-shirts said A, R, and F, respectively. It made R so happy and the sun shone a little brighter upon the world that day.

Have we stopped talking about this since then? No. We still do, but R knows now how fortunate he's to have friends that are different from him in all imaginable ways and yet they share this innocent bond of friendship and brotherhood.

Richa Dinesh Sharma lives in Singapore with her husband, two human children, and one furchild. Her poems have featured in well-known international literary journals FineLines Winter 2021 edition (and upcoming Spring 2022), OpenDoor Poetry magazine, Our Poetry Archives and some anthologies. Occasionally, as inspiration strikes, she writes in Hindi, *"Hindi fostered my love of reading and writing while English indulged me like an aunt"*. She dabbles in Art when not writing or daydreaming. At present, she is working remotely as an editor of the reputed quarterly FineLines Literary Journal based out of Omaha, USA. On Instagram @dryink_brush, email: richa.soul@gmail.com

I saw growth in my child when...

_____

_____

_____

_____

_____

_____

_____

_____

_____

_____

_____

_____

_____

_____

_____

_____

_____

_____

_____

_____

Darryl Varnado

The Talk, a Grandfather's Perspective

The year is 1971. In a small southern town east of the Mississippi River, a young Black man is sprinting down the street in the evening. He is late for his last date with his girlfriend prior to returning to college out of state, and he is eager to arrive as quickly as possible. About a mile outside of his neighborhood, he is stopped by the six white policemen in four patrol cars that happen by. He is questioned: What's your name? Where are you going? Why are you running? Where are you coming from?

This young man, being Black, knows full well the one and only reason he has been stopped. Being proud, and being young, he declines to answer their questions. He ends up being taken into custody. He could have ended up dead!

This is my story. That young man was me. But this story is far from unique. I daresay that every Black family in America has its own version. Change the date. Change the town. Change the names. This story has been played out, and continues to play, every day across these United States. And not every time is the person "lucky" enough to have only been detained. Every Black person knows

The Talk

what I'm talking about. And we know that there will come a day when we need to give our children—especially our sons—"the talk."

If you are white and you give your child the talk, you are telling them about the birds and the bees. If you are a person of color, you are telling them how to stay out of harm's way. If you are white, you may be thinking, "People of color aren't the only ones who have been stopped by the police for no apparent reason." That may be true. But what is also true is that if you are white, you will never be stopped because of your skin color.

As parents we walk a fine line between teaching our children to be strong and independent and staying out of situations where this strength and independence could get them in trouble. So I have had to tell my grandsons to acquiesce when approached by law enforcement, even when they know they are being wronged. I have told them that policemen and policewomen across the country are said to "serve and protect." But who are they serving and who are they protecting? In far too many cases, it is not those whose skin is not white.

The talk that I have given to my grandsons is the same talk that my father gave to me. Simply because your skin has been beautifully kissed by the sun, it will cause you to be singled out for undeserved attention or even punishment.

The Talk

But I take care in my talks with my grandsons, to caution them that while they may hear Black men referred to as an "endangered" or even a "dying species," they can choose whether to see their glass as being half full or half empty. That is pretty much the way it is with most things in life. The Black man, an "endangered species?" Let me respond by saying that MY glass is always half full. It has to be, lest I die of thirst twice as quickly.

The talk that I heard as a young man did not come only from my father. It also came from my mother... from my pastors, my teachers, my coaches, my mentors... and from a myriad of people in the broader community that know that they must look out for their own. In the same way that I have been encouraged but also cautioned, I have encouraged my grandsons to see that their glass is always at least half full. But while I'm loving in my intent, I am blunt in my expressions and stern in my speech. I tell them that the playing field, no matter how level it may look, is not always what it appears. It doesn't matter that they attend good schools or are in classes with a diverse student population. They are still young Black men. It doesn't matter if their parents are CEOs of a major corporation or bus drivers. They are still young Black men. And that when they walk into a store, or a classroom, or into a job interview, or even just sprinting down the street, the first thing that too many people will see is not that they are intelligent, or educated, or well-mannered, but that they are Black. And even some of those people who do acknowledge their virtues will believe that they are somehow an anomaly, an exception to the rule.

So, I have told my grandsons that when—not if, but when—they are pulled over by the police, they are to speak respectfully, keep their hands visible, and preface their movements with an explanation of what they are about to do. (Had I followed my own father's advice on that evening 1971, I would not have ended up at that police station!) I instruct them to be mindful of how the police, their teachers, and many white people in general may see them as older than their actual years and bigger than their actual size. They will be seen as threatening.

Black parents have an obligation to protect their children in ways that others in our society take for granted. It breaks my heart, especially fifty years after my own encounter with the police, to have to have this conversation with innocent children. No parent should be required to have that conversation with their child or grandchild. It is talks of encouragement and reminders that their glass is half full. It is talks to make sure that they have a fighting chance of never becoming part of that "endangered species." It's the talks that are laced with the same strong, emotional language I heard from the whole village of my community: Preachers, teachers, neighbors and most importantly, my parents. It is words of wisdom to keep them on the path of righteousness, to keep them safe; moreover, to keep them alive. We are challenged on all fronts, but that doesn't mean that we will not conquer. I take tremendous care not to break my grandsons' spirit, but I want them to come home safely at the end of the day.

Too many people assume that because our young men are Black, their glasses are half empty. Our job as their parents and mentors is to show them that their glass is half full, no matter what others may think, and to teach them how to fill it to the brim.

How I view life is my story. How I got to my station in life is my story. How I help my grandsons to reach their potential is my story as well. I have a story to tell, and it is an important one. But it's not the one that I am sharing with you today. The most important one I have already told, and will keep on telling, to my grandsons.

Finally, after much reflection, the question remains: why? Why is this talk still an urgent and necessary part of life in Black families? Why is it needed in America, the land of the free and the home of the brave? I will tell you why: it is because we are neither free nor brave. Our minds are not free. Too many in this country still have beliefs of supremacy based on skin color. Martin Luther King Jr. said it simply, and profoundly: "No one is free until we are all free." We are not brave. Too many of us are cowards, fearfully believing the mistaken notion that in order for some to excel, others must fail. Fear motivates most of the cruelties in our world, said Maya Angelou. "Courage," she continued, "is the most important of all the virtues, because without courage you can't practice any other virtues consistently." To be that thing in your heart, you have to have courage.

The talk will continue to be a necessary part of life in Black families until white families have a talk with their children as well. Teaching children about racism is not the sole responsibility of people of color. Rather, the talk that well-meaning white parents must have is not the "colorblind" approach that minimizes the significance of race. Many white parents say, "We don't stress race to our children because we want them to learn that the color of one's skin doesn't matter." This failure to focus on color results in a failure to see our own discrimination. And one cannot fight what one does not see. The first step is the urgent need for all American parents to have "straight talks" with their children that acknowledge the existence of systemic racism. Only then can we even begin to instill in our children, black and white, the courage to dispel the fear that feeds the cruelty of racism. Only then can we live up to the ideals of Mahatma Gandhi and "be the change you wish to see in the world."

Darryl Varnado is a retired human resources executive with extensive experience as Chief People Officer at two academic medical centers and several other industries. He was recognized as a Minority Business Leader by the Washington Business Journal in 2016. Varnado was also selected in 2019 as the Chief Human Resources Officer (CHRO) of the Year, by HRO Today. Varnado resides in Falls Church, Virginia, USA.

"Be the change you wish to see in the world."

Mahatma Gandhi - What is your wish?

_____

_____

_____

_____

_____

_____

_____

_____

_____

_____

_____

_____

_____

_____

_____

_____

_____

_____

_____

_____

_____

The Talk

Lyris D. Wallace

Living While Black

The greatest day of my life was the day I welcomed my son into this world. Like most moms with children, I felt like I blinked and suddenly my newborn had become a grown man. Time seemed to fly by. It never seems like enough time to share all there is about life and how to maneuver through it, with as little damage as possible, especially growing up as a black male child with only a divorced mom leading the way. I found myself talking long and talking often. Not because my son was difficult, but simply because he was black and I knew the world would see him, not as the cute little boy I saw him as, but as a threat and something that needed to be gotten under control.

As my son grew older and more independent, I became more vocal and told him how to move in a world where certain people would find his very presence intimidating. "When you're walking downtown, son, always walk as if you have somewhere to be. Never stroll or walk slowly, never linger too long in front of a business, and only enter in if you have money in your pocket and you are ready to make a purchase. Most of all keep your hands where they can be seen and never put your hoodie up, not even if it's raining."

The Talk

It was quite difficult for me because my experience growing up was different from my son's. First of all, I was a black female, who grew up in the white suburbs outside of the big city, under the watchful eye of a very intimidating father and a very wise mother. My son grew up in the inner city of Chicago, under the watchful eye of a single, divorced mom. I had to learn quickly and I had to relay those lessons to him without scaring him and without letting society make him feel less than or that he was something to be feared and controlled. I remember when my son had a school assembly and the Chicago Police came to speak to the children about how the police were there to help them and if they saw any trouble or felt like they were in danger to notify the police and they would be there to help them.

When Jonah came home and told me about that assembly I first felt angry. How could they stand there and lie to those precious black children's faces? And then I felt sad, because I had to explain to my son, that wasn't true for us as black people. "Police are not your friend son, they are your accuser. If you feel threatened, run to the closest black adult you can find. If you see a crime being committed and are questioned by the police, the only answer you give is 'I didn't see anything sir.' Then you give them my name and my phone number. I don't care if the crime happened right in front of you, you say you saw nothing, because they will try to implicate you in it somehow."

The Talk

One of the scariest days for me, while raising my son, was the first day of sophomore year when he was 15 years old. My son came home so happy and excited as he threw down a book on the coffee table. He said, "Oh mama, this is going to be a great year!!" I said, feeling his excitement too, "yeah? And why is that, son?" He looked at me all wide eyed, with a big grin on his face, and said the two most dreaded words you could hear as the mother of growing black boy in an urban city, "DRIVER'S ED" I'm taking driver's education this semester and soon I'll have my license." When he said those words, I could swear I heard them in slow motion. My mouth went dry, my heart pounded like a bass drum, and I got hot all over. I didn't want to quell his enthusiasm with my fear, but I had to tell him there were rules he needed to follow, that were not in that Rules of the Road book he threw on the coffee table.

Rule #1, never drive with more than one other person in the car with you. I know you have a lot of friends, but cops like to pull over cars that have lots of black males inside. 2. If you should get pulled over, KEEP BOTH HANDS ON THE WHEEL. If they ask you for your license, ask them if you have permission to retrieve it from your back pocket. 3. While the cop is running your license, tell your passenger to remain quiet and to turn on their camera phone. 4. If asked to get out of the car, say "you do not have my permission to search my car, I do not have any drugs or weapons of any kind in my car." 5. Do not engage with them, stick to 'yes sir/no sir' and above all, STAY CALM."

These are just a few of the talks I have had with my son Jonah as he grew up and now that he is a 21 year old man, I still talk because it is still necessary. It's even more necessary now that he is a man than it was when he was a boy. Now I have to explain to him, why when he's finally a man at 21 he will more than likely be referred to, by his white boss as a boy, but when he was 17 he was called a man.

As black mothers we must never stop talking to our black children, especially our black sons. We must talk long and we must talk often.

Lyris D. Wallace is a Literary visionary. Reared in the South Suburbs outside Chicago. African American Literature influenced her writing and is one of her favorite genres. Wallace writes in the spirit of her past great Literary ancestors. 2022 garnered Lyris her very first literary nomination, Pushcart Nominee-Poem *No Justice for Breonna*, Published in "Social Justice Inks" Anthology.

Along with her sister, Chyrel J. Jackson, they published "Mirrored Images" and "Different Sides of the Same Coin." This edgy writing duo appears in over 8 published poetry Anthologies. You will find them always writing. Creating written legacies one book at a time.

Wallace is one writer that has found her poetic voice. You can find her on Sistersrocnrhyme.com

My definition of freedom is...

_____
_____
_____
_____
_____
_____
_____
_____
_____
_____
_____
_____
_____
_____
_____
_____
_____
_____
_____
_____
_____
_____
_____

The Talk

What is your story?

Would you like to share your vital conversations, essays, poems, or other expressions? Now is as good a time as any to get started.

On the next few pages are the beginnings of journal pages to record your words.

The Talk does not end here. This is a good place to start sharing your words.

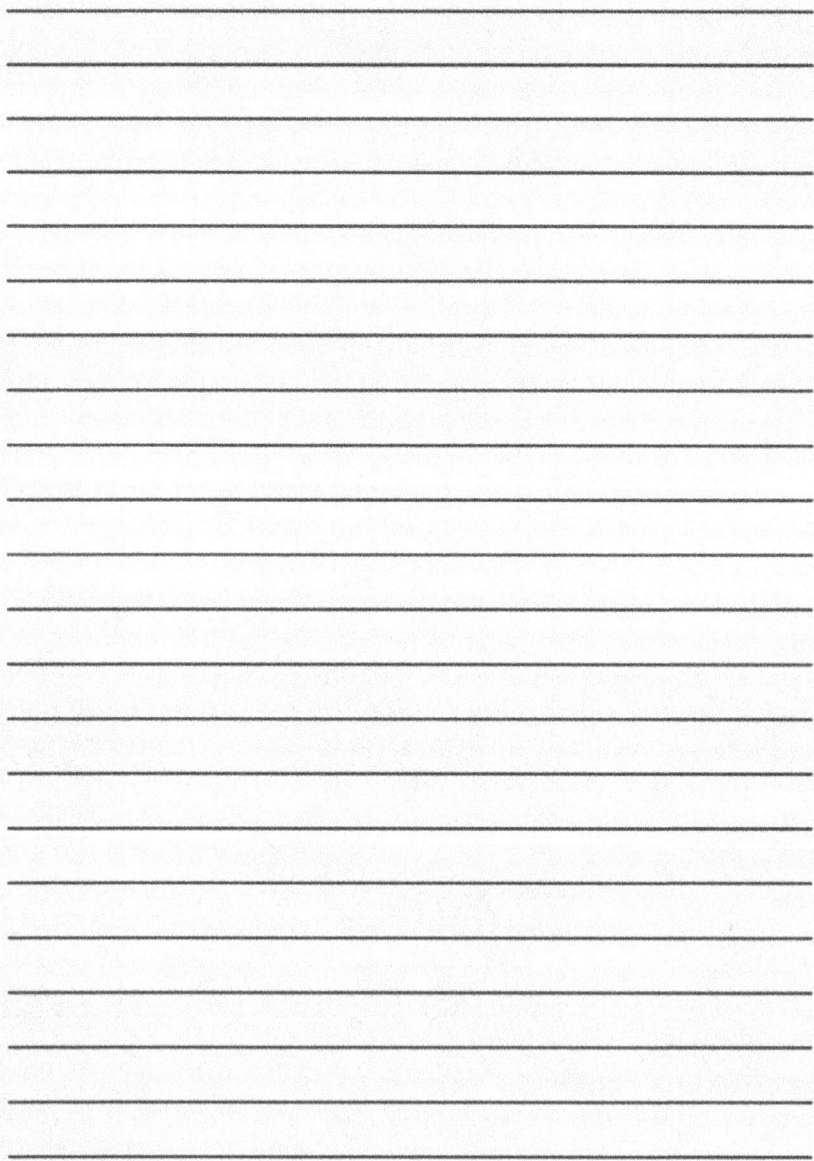

What's Next?

These essays, poems, and vital discussions need to continue.

Do you have experiences you would like to share?

Please go to GardenofNeuro.com and select "Keep the Talk Going" and add your thoughts.

This is a dialogue that will continue as long as we keep talking.

**Scan to Go to
Garden of Neuro
Calls for Submissions**

Resources

She is on point and always has relevant content:
vernamyers.com/
※
janeelliott.com/
※
Peruse this site and note this particular article:
goodblacknews.org/?s=white+privilege
※
"America Forced Me To Have 'The Talk' With My Black Child Before I Was Ready"

huffpost.com/entry/the-talk-parents-of-black-kids_n_5ee0039dc5b6716df298adaa
※
National SEED Project (Seeking Educational Equity and Diversity), Peggy McIntosh: "White Privilege, Unpacking the Invisible Knapsack"
※

Peggy McIntosh TED Talk: "How to recognize your white privilege — and use it to fight inequality"
※
Diversity, Equity, and Inclusion (DEI) defined:
dei.extension.org/

The Talk

A Mighty Long Way: My Journey to Justice at Little Rock Central High School
by Carlotta Walls LaNier (Author), Lisa Frazier Page (Author), Bill Clinton (Contributor)
※
"What is White Privilege Really?" by Cory Collins
learningforjustice.org/magazine/fall-2018/what-is-white-privilege-really
※
Center for Equity & Excellence
rosemarieallen.com/
※
International Early Childhood Inclusion Institute:
inclusioninstitute.fpg.unc.edu/presenters/allen-rosemarie
※
DEI Strategy: Converge Firm:
convergefirm.com/about
※
GardenofNeuro.com will also have these links and continue to add resource information.

GARDEN OF NEURO INSTITUTE

If you would like to explore more about the

Garden of Neuro Institute, go to:

Garden of Neuro.com

www.ingramcontent.com/pod-product-compliance
Lightning Source LLC
Chambersburg PA
CBHW052111090426

42741CB00009B/1765